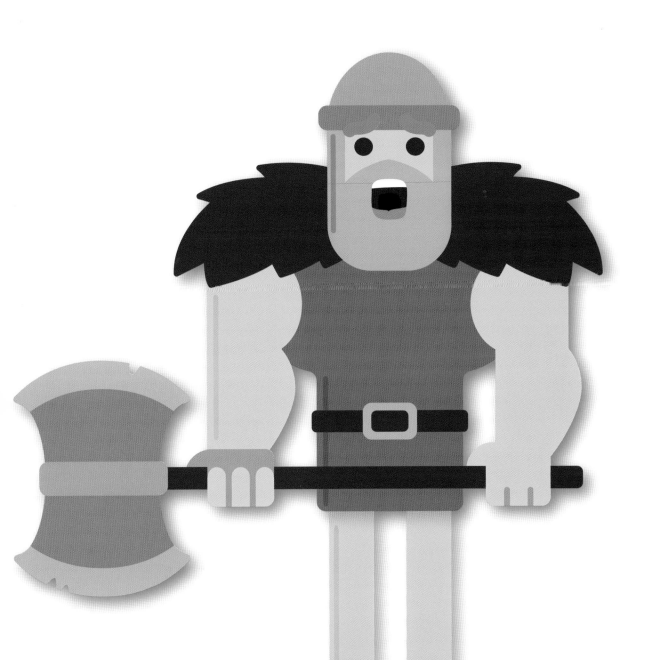

PEOPLE DID WHAT?
IN THE
VIKING AGE

By Shalini Vallepur

BookLife
PUBLISHING

©2019
BookLife Publishing Ltd.
King's Lynn
Norfolk, PE30 4LS

All rights reserved.
Printed in Malaysia.

A catalogue record for this
book is available from the
British Library.

ISBN: 978-1-78637-861-3

With thanks to Robin Twiddy, William Anthony
and Emilie Dufresne.

Written by:
Shalini Vallepur

Edited by:
Madeline Tyler

Designed by:
Dan Scase

Are you ready to learn all about the Viking Age, and what we Vikings got up to?

PHOTO CREDITS

CONTENTS

Words that look like **THIS** are explained in the glossary on page 31.

Welcome to the Viking Age!

Heilsa! This is how people used to greet each other in the language spoken by the Vikings – Old Norse. The Viking Age was a time roughly between the years AD 800 and 1066.

Viking area

WHO WERE THE VIKINGS?

Vikings were part of a group of people from <u>SCANDINAVIA</u>, called Norsemen. The Norsemen who went out on <u>RAIDS</u> and made their homes around Europe were called Vikings. Most Vikings were Norse farmers or <u>BLACKSMITHS</u> who became fierce warriors when they were needed to go out on raids.

FACT
The name 'Viking' comes from an Old Norse word that used to mean 'raiding'.

VIKING SETTLEMENTS

Vikings built villages and towns wherever they travelled. Jarls, or earls, were important people who owned land, ships and treasure. A jarl was usually a rich man or a great warrior.

An ordinary person was called a karl. A karl was usually a farmer, blacksmith or other craftsman. A karl was a freeman who was allowed to own land. A thrall was somebody who wasn't free and couldn't own land – usually a <u>SLAVE</u>.

A lot of people think that we were horrible people, and we were in some ways. However, we also did a lot of nice things too! Read on and find out what we did.

FACT
The Vikings are sometimes known as the Danes.

Raiding, Trading and Exploring

Scandinavia was a lovely place to live, but many Norsemen were bored with being farmers and blacksmiths. They wanted more land, more riches and the thrills of life as a Viking. Besides, it was all too easy for us to set sail and get rich by going on raids because nobody was expecting us.

TO THE LONGSHIP!

We built wooden longships to sail the sea. Some were shaped like dragons. They were long, strong, speedy and perfect for storing LOOT from raids.

Did you shut the gate, then?

It's too late.

We raided many MONASTERIES in Britain. They had barely any defences.

Oars were used to help the ship move without wind.

Dragon or monster heads on the PROW of the ship scared off enemies.

A big woollen sail caught the wind and pushed the boat along.

All aboard!

FACT
Important Vikings were often buried in their ships.

TRADE

Raiding was a lot of fun, but we also traded goods. This meant that we gave Viking things to other people and they gave us some of their things in return. Thanks to our longships, we were able to sail along rivers in Europe and Central Asia and meet all kinds of people. Sometimes, people didn't want to trade with us, but that was fine. We could take them to be slaves back home, or sell them!

Now we're in a whole new world.

I'll give you one bit of silk for the slave.

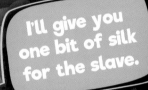

Hmm, make that two bits of silk.

LEIF DID WHAT?

Leif Erikson took Vikings to a whole new world – literally! In AD 1000, it is believed that Leif sailed from Greenland to North America. He is believed to be the first Viking – and the first European – to ever set foot on the **CONTINENT** of North America, but he didn't stay there for long.

The Great Gods

We believed in many gods and goddesses during the Viking Age. Whilst we lived on Earth, or Midgard, the gods lived in a place called Asgard. Each god looked after a certain part of life.

Here are a few of the main gods and goddesses that we worshipped:

Odin (Óðinn) – King of Asgard, god of war, poetry and magic

Thor (Þórr) – God of thunder and strength, son of Odin and Frigg, loud, proud and carries a mighty hammer called Mjöllnir

Freyja – Goddess of love and beauty, twin sister of Freyr

Loki – From the land of giants, a mischievous god who plays tricks on the gods in Asgard

Freyr – God of farming, twin brother of Freyja

Frigg – Queen of Asgard, protector of children

Balder (Baldr) – God of light and purity, killed by Hodr who was tricked by Loki

Tyr – God of war and justice

WORSHIP

We had to keep the gods and goddesses happy by <u>WORSHIPPING</u> them. In order to keep Odin happy, some Vikings made <u>SACRIFICES</u> to him. The sacrifices were usually animals, but sometimes people were sacrificed too.

Step right up, step right up. Who wants to be sacrificed first?

Vikings stopped sacrificing people when they started to follow Christianity.

THOR DID WHAT?

Thor loved his hammer Mjöllnir very much, so you can imagine how upset he was when it was stolen by Thrym the giant. Thrym said that he would give Mjöllnir back if he could marry Freyja, but Freyja refused. Thor would do anything for Mjöllnir — even pretend to be Freyja...

With the help of Loki, Thor was dressed as a beautiful bride. Thrym didn't realise that his bride 'Freyja' was really Thor, even when Thor ate an entire ox, eight fish and drank many barrels of <u>MEAD</u>. When Mjöllnir was brought out, Thor immediately grabbed it and killed Thrym. Don't mess with Thor!

What beautiful eyes you have!

Precious Pets

Vikings kept all sorts of animals as pets, but some were more ferocious than others...

BABY BEARS

Some families kept bears as pets. Baby bears were taken and raised alongside people. Some were <u>TAME</u>, but most of them caused a lot of trouble. If a bear got loose and hurt anybody, the owner would have to pay a <u>FINE</u> as a punishment.

Karls had brown bears, but the jarls got their hands on polar bears. Polar bears were brought to Scandinavia on longships.

UNICORNS?

We didn't keep unicorns as pets, but we traded their horns. Yes, I swear we did. Oh, OK, you got me. So, we may have lied about unicorns to traders. We pretended that narwhal teeth were unicorn horns and sold them to people who believed that they were magical.

Narwhal tooth

She's real, I swear.

DUTIFUL DOGS

Lots of Vikings kept dogs as pets for hunting and guarding. Dogs were expensive to keep. The more dogs somebody had, the richer they were.

My precious pooch!

Some Vikings even took their dogs with them on raids. It was believed that dogs could follow their masters to the **AFTERLIFE**.

PRETTY PEACOCKS

The richest Vikings kept peacocks as pets. They were **IMPORTED** and were so fancy that people made **BROOCHES** in the shape of peacocks.

Show me off to all your friends.

Let's Go Berserk

Out in the forest, where nobody else went, lived the berserkers. You wouldn't want to mess with one of them — they were more animal than man. They had special connections to the god Odin and animals such as the bear and the wolf. The berserkers would eat, drink and sleep just like an animal. Some even walked about naked except for the animal skins on their back.

Charge!

Someone's hungry!

IT'S ALL THE RAGE

Berserkers went into a **TRANCE** and lost control of themselves. This was called 'berserkergang'. Their teeth chattered, they shivered uncontrollably and their faces changed colour. They were terrifying and driven by rage and **BLOODLUST**.

Some berserkers were so blinded by their bloodlust that they bit their shields!

THE BEAR BERSERKER

Bear berserkers believed that they had the spirit of a bear within them. They would fight anybody who came into their way. King Olaf made a huge mistake when he put berserkers at the front of his army – in their blind rage the berserkers ran ahead of everybody else, leaving the others unprotected. This ended in King Olaf losing the battle. Big mistake!

Leave me alone!

Arghhhhhh!

Is it a bear? Is it a man? Or is it a berserker?

THE WOLF BERSERKER

Wolf berserkers had a connection to wolves. They terrified everybody in a battle by howling and barking as if they were mad wolves. When they weren't ripping people to shreds on the battlefield, they were trying their best to become wolves. Some berserkers drank the blood of wolves in an attempt to make themselves as wolfish as possible.

Awooooooo!

The Life of a Child

NO WEAKNESS ALLOWED

Everybody had to be strong in order to be a Viking. If a baby didn't look strong or became sick, their parents would leave them outside to die.

Mum?

LIFE IN THE LONGHOUSE

When they weren't off on raids, most Vikings lived in small farming COMMUNITIES out in the countryside. Children grew up alongside their family and farm animals in houses called longhouses. A longhouse had one big room. There was a big fire pit in the middle for cooking and warmth and everybody slept on benches around it.

At the back of the longhouse, there was a barn for CATTLE and horses to live in. Things were a bit smelly, smoky and cramped, but we got along most of the time.

FACT
Some longhouses were so big that 50 people could live inside!

Longhouse

14

OFF TO WORK

Wait, you want me to put this up where?

Viking children didn't go to school. They learnt everything they needed from their parents. Boys and girls helped with cooking, <u>WEAVING</u> and working on the farm. Boys, and some girls, were taught how to fight using swords, spears and axes, so that they were ready to fight in wars and go on raids.

Boys and girls were thought of as adults when they were around 10 years old.

TERRIFIC TOYS

When they weren't busy working, Viking children had all sorts of wooden toys to play with, from dolls and swords to boats and board games.

Hnefatafl was a game played by lots of Vikings. There were two players. One player had 16 pieces and had to attack the other player's 8 pieces to capture the other player's king. This game was a perfect way to practise battle <u>TACTICS</u>!

King

Runes

Whenever we needed to write things down, we used runes. Runes were carved onto big stones as well as onto weapons and jewellery. Most people could read runes.

Big stones like these had the names of brave warriors and heroes carved onto them.

This had better be worth it.

RUNES DID WHAT?

Runes were magical. We believed that Odin discovered the runes when he hung himself from the world tree for nine days. The world tree was a giant tree from many Viking stories – it was at the centre of the universe, and the gods would often visit it. Thanks to Odin's sacrifice, runes had magical powers. They were used for good and bad.

Curse you, Björn, for leaving the seat up.

Not everybody could use the magical powers of runes. A seeress was a special woman who would go into a trance and use runes to look into the future or CURSE somebody. Runes were written onto little pieces of wood or bone. The seeress would throw the runes on the floor and then look at how they landed to see what was in store for that person.

Rune stones

Some Vikings carved runes onto their weapons so that they would be stronger in battle.

THE GRAFFITI SAYS WHAT?

We used runes for all sorts of things. Some people used runes to write their names or rude messages on walls, a bit like <u>GRAFFITI</u>.

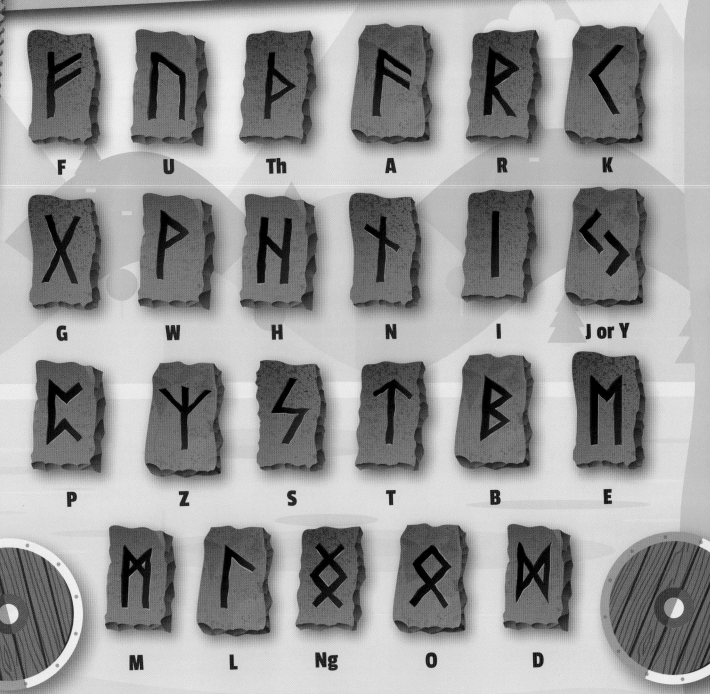

F U Th A R K

G W H N I J or Y

P Z S T B E

M L Ng O D

It looks like someone has carved a message for me! What does it say? I hope it's nice!

Very Viking Feasts

We held big feasts to celebrate **FESTIVALS** as well as weddings and successful raids. Everybody would gather in a big longhouse. Feasts were the best – we had lots of food to go around and huge tubs full of mead.

Longhouse

FACT
Some feasts went on for 12 days!

We drank mead out of animal horns like this.

Let's go to the feast. It'll be fun, I promise...

FAREWELL HORSEY

Sacrificing animals before a feast happened a lot. The sacrifice was done in the name of the gods. If somebody wanted to prove that they loved the gods, they would sacrifice their favourite horse.

We didn't just eat at a feast. There was lots of entertainment to keep everybody happy: from music and games, to the flyting. I loved a good flyting. People came together to call each other names and just be rude to each other! It wasn't all shouting and being rude though — people had to be clever and poetic during a flyting if they wanted to be the winner.

CHECK OUT MY FLYTING

Check out my flyting, you're all super boring. Sacrificed my horse, now I can't go prancing. I got Thor on my side, watch out for his lightning. Very, very frightening.

LOKI DID WHAT?

The gods had their own flytings too, and Loki was especially mean to the other gods. Loki killed a servant at a feast and angered everyone. He began a flyting and started calling the other gods names. When the others chased after Loki, Loki turned into a salmon and tried to swim away, but the other gods caught him in a net and tied him to a rock. A giant snake dripped poison onto Loki's face... forever.

THE PUNISHMENT OF LOKI.

Fun and Games

FANCY A SWIM?

We enjoyed lots of sports and games in between farming, raiding and sailing. We loved competitions. One of my favourite competitions was a swimming game. The aim of the game was to hold your OPPONENT under water for as long as you could. If they drowned, then it was their fault!

Ah, the perfect place for a little swimming competition...

TUG OF WAR

Tug of war was a great game that also tested strength. Using a rope made from animal skin, two teams had to pull the rope to see which team was stronger. There was one catch – if you lost and fell forwards, you would probably die because the game was played over a burning fire!

LET'S SKI...

Whenever it was too snowy to travel by horse or boat, skiing was the way to go. We made our skis out of wood. They were perfect for zooming down hills and made hunting easy.

... AND SKATE!

Last one to the bottom of the hill smells!

Weeeee!

We used bones to make skates. Horse, cow or ELK bones were best. We attached the bones to shoes and used the skates to glide across frozen lakes. Sometimes, we used sticks to pull and push ourselves forwards over the ice.

21

Þing

Most Vikings took the <u>LAW</u> into their own hands by fighting each other. But there were so many Viking settlements and communities all over Europe that we needed a good way to solve problems, arrange marriages and just have a good gossip. So, each community had their own 'Þing' to discuss issues and sort out any problems.

Some laws were written down like this, but usually laws were <u>MEMORISED</u> by someone called a law-speaker.

Do you remember what the rune 'Þ' sounds like? Turn back to page 17 to find out.

Viking Þings were big meetings. Freemen went to the meetings along with jarls and other important Vikings. I loved going to a Þing because you got to decide what happened to criminals and other wrongdoers. Most criminals were given fines, which were a lot better than some of the other punishments we had.

All in favour, say aye. All against, say nay.

Nay.

OUTLAW

Some criminals became outlaws. This meant that they were <u>BANISHED</u> from the community. Everything was taken from them; they had no house, no weapons, no food and no help from anybody. It was a dangerous world out there.

Goodbye, everybody. It was nice knowing you.

GRETTIR DID WHAT?

Grettir was a famous outlaw who survived as an outlaw for 20 years! Look here. Was this stone written on by Grettir? Let's read it and see what happened...

Grettir

Dear Diary, I miss my cosy longhouse. I hate being an outlaw. I didn't mean to kill everybody in that fire. They took everything from me, even my favourite comb. I am terribly lonely, but I'm not alone – there are people chasing me. Apparently, they have every right to kill me just because I'm an outlaw! But they won't catch me; I'll keep travelling around the world killing monsters and hopefully they'll start being nice to me.

HOLMGANG

A lot of people sorted out their issues and arguments with holmgang. Holmgang was a type of duel, which is a fight between two people. The first person to bleed was the loser.

Winning a holmgang proved that you were right and that the gods were on your side. I've won a few holmgangs in my time.

Bring it on.

It wasn't unusual for a holmgang to be a fight to the death.

Some holmgangs took place in a longhouse, but a lot of them took place where nobody else could get in the way. Some took place on tiny islands. That way if somebody chickened out, they couldn't run away.

The perfect place for a holmgang

THE BLOOD EAGLE

There was an awful punishment that was only carried out a few times. It was called the blood eagle. A person's back was cut and their ribs were pulled out. It looked like they were a bird. I'm glad I've never seen one.

Ah, it's so horrible! Maybe that's why everybody thought we were horrible people...

TO FLOAT OR NOT TO FLOAT

We had lots of ways to find out whether somebody was INNOCENT or not. For some crimes, we would tie the person up and throw them out into a lake. If they floated then they were GUILTY and burnt alive. If they sank and drowned it was because they were innocent. They still died, but at least we knew they were innocent.

So it looks like I was innocent after all... Blub, blub...

Keeping Clean

A lot of people thought that Vikings were a smelly bunch, but they're wrong! We kept very clean, thank you very much! We had a bath once a week and we washed our faces every day, which was a lot more than some stinky people who only washed once a year.

Some Vikings bathed in **HOT SPRING** baths like this.

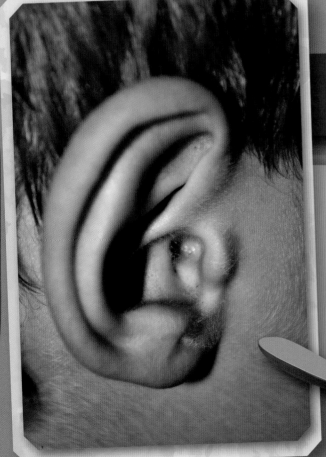

DON'T FORGET THE EARS!

We didn't just bathe, we kept all parts of ourselves clean. We had special spoons and picks for our ears. They were made of bone or wood and we used them to pick and scoop out earwax.

This Wee Is on Fire

Because we travelled a lot, we needed to make sure that we were prepared for anything. We had one very special way of making fire that involved lots of wee.

First we took a tinder mushroom and cut it up into slices. Then we burnt it a little so that it turned black. Finally, we took a pot of wee and boiled the burned mushroom strips in it. This made the perfect, stinky material that could be used to start a fire!

Tinder mushroom

Hair Care and Fashion

Hair care was important to Vikings. A lot of men wanted to have lighter or blonder hair, so they used a special soap to turn their hair lighter. Beards were also important and some men lightened their beards as well. Some men had such great hair and beards that they became a part of their names!

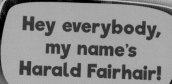

Hey everybody, my name's Harald Fairhair!

COOL COMBS

FACT
A Viking law said that women weren't allowed to cut their hair short.

We carried combs wherever we went so that we always looked good. A fierce warrior wouldn't go anywhere without a sword, knife and comb. Our combs were very pretty as well – we carved all sorts of patterns on them. Some Vikings were buried with their combs too, so they could look neat and tidy in the afterlife.

HARALD DID WHAT?

Decorating teeth was very popular in the Viking Age. We carved lines onto our teeth, and it is thought that some people would fill the lines with <u>DYE</u> so their smiles would be happy and colourful!

Harald Bluetooth was the King of Denmark. He got his name from his blue teeth. I never met Harald Bluetooth so I'm not sure if he carved and dyed his teeth or if he just ate too many blueberries.

29

Far Vel!

Far vel! That means 'farewell' in Old Norse. Did anything surprise you about the Vikings? I hope you learnt lots of new things about us.

Do you think you would have enjoyed living during the Viking Age? Would you have been a bear or a wolf berserker? Or maybe you would have preferred to sail the seas and explore the world? Life in the Viking Age was fun as long as you didn't get caught in a holmgang!

GLOSSARY

AFTERLIFE a religious belief that there is life after death

BANISHED to be banned from somewhere and never allowed to return

BLACKSMITHS people who make things out of metal

BLOODLUST feeling the need to be violent towards others

BROOCHES pieces of jewellery that can be pinned onto clothing

CATTLE cows, bulls and oxen

COMMUNITIES groups of people who live and work together

CONTINENT a large area of land, such as Africa or Europe, that is made up of many countries

CURSE to give someone bad luck or misfortune, often through magic or spells

DYE a liquid that can change the colour of fabric

ELK large deer that are found in northern Europe and Asia

FESTIVALS celebrations held to honour something or someone

FINE a sum of money that someone has to pay for doing something wrong

GRAFFITI pictures or words that are drawn or written, without permission, onto a public place such as a wall or building

GUILTY responsible for a specific bad action or wrongdoing

HOT SPRING a body of water that is naturally warm

IMPORTED brought in from another place

INNOCENT not responsible for, or guilty of, something

LAW a rule set by a certain area or country

LOOT things that are taken or stolen after an attack

MEAD an alcoholic drink made of honey

MEMORISED remembered perfectly

MONASTERIES the buildings in which monks and sometimes nuns live

OPPONENT the person you are fighting against

PROW the pointed part at the front of a ship

RAIDS sudden or surprise attacks

SACRIFICES animals, people or things that are killed or destroyed as an offering to a god or gods

SCANDINAVIA the northern part of Europe that includes the countries of Norway, Sweden, Denmark, Finland and Iceland

SLAVE a person who has no freedom and is owned by another person

TACTICS plans or methods for achieving a certain goal

TAME when an animal is gentle and calm around people

TRANCE a state that seems to be between being asleep and awake in which people might act differently to usual

WEAVING using threads to make fabric

WORSHIPPING performing a religious act to express respect for a god or gods

INDEX

Rune message (page 17): YOU SMELL LIKE POO